Life Expectancy
Previously Unpublished Poems from the 1980s

by Ken Jones

Editing and Selecting by
Dustin Pickering and Z.M. Wise

This anthology is © Transcendent Zero Press, 2018. Each work belongs to Ken Jones and may not be reproduced, whether electronically or in print, without the expressed consent of the publisher or the author.

PUBLISHED BY TRANSCENDENT ZERO PRESS

www.transcendentzeropress.org

ISBN-13: 978-1-946460-00-4

ISBN-10: 1946460-00-1

Printed in the United States of America

Library of Congress Control Number: 2018937916

All Poetry © 2018 Ken Jones

All Rights Reserved

Cover Design — "Ken Jones Seduced by the Miser," by Susie Tommaney, based on the painting, *Death and the Miser*, by Hieronymus Bosch

FIRST EDITION

TRANSCENDENT ZERO PRESS

Table of Contents

Epigraph 3

Organic Inertia 4

Birthright 5

Manroot and Rosebud 6

Survival of the Litter Runt 7

Severe Storm Warnings in Effect 8

Natural Structure 9

Life Expectancy 10

Corporate Park I 11

The Tenneco Tower Throws Cold Shadows 12

Crank Case 13

American Trends: The End? 14

A Hungry Anger 15

The Science of Silence 16

Knowledgeable Idiots 17

Encyclopedia Humanum is Missing Many Volumes 18

Feels Almost Human 19

Nothing Human Is Foreign to Me 20

Hydrocarbon Blues 21

Behind the Register at a Convenience Store 22

Planned Obsolescence 23

Wooden Man 24

Infinite Sameness 25

Desperate Stairs 26

Innocent Piss 27

A Unique Vision? 28

Speechless Statis Slept Here 29

Crummy Rummage 30

We Walk the Line 31

Fear Reified 32

Microorganisms 33

Psychomachea 34

What the Bible Contains 35

White Witch Hollow 36

Manufactured Disaster 37

The Established Couple 38

Emergence as Raw Experience 39

What Means Much 40

On the Creation of Artificial Environments 41

The Conversion of Wallace Stevens 42

The Consent of the Governed 43

The American Way! 44

Sister Cindy	45
The Status Quo is my Hero	46
The Order of Things	47
The Condemned Complex	48
The Wave	49
The Hairy Ape	50
The Reigning Monarch	51
Another Cold Soldier	52
Black Beauty	53
Teasing	54
Disneyland of Death	55
In the American Train	56
A Little Like Hilarity Hall	57
Nutty	58
The "Great Apes" of History	59
Economic Reality	60
On Killing Living Things	61
Rack 'Em Up	62
Sermons on the Random	63
The Literature of Exhaustion	65

Introduction to Life Expectancy

After numerous discussions over the past few years with poets, musicians and artists I respect, the topic of unpublished work has come to haunt me as I enter the September of my years.

What is someone's "Life's Work?" How is it quantified or judged — if at all — when the artist is living or dead?

In the midst of many life changes over the past three years, I began to assemble and reassemble my poetry, prose, music, plays, screenplays, movies, videos, etc. into Rubbermaid® containers for security and eventual transport to my creative archive at the University of Texas at Brownsville. This process has led me to conclude that some of my best work has yet to see publication in any format. This book of some unpublished poems from my college and graduate school days at the University of Texas at Austin is my first — hopefully not my last — attempt to address the broader issue.

Thanks to Dustin Pickering of Transcendent Zero Press who had asked, "to see any manuscript you have" for his support and friendship. Also a shout-out to his cohort Z.M. Wise who lived up to his last name. And a special thanks to Susie Tommaney for her clever cover art, typing and graphic design skills.

I believe these poems stand the test of time. I hope any readers here agree.

Ken Jones
March 2018
Gonzales, Texas

Epigraph

The air is full of farewells to the dying.
And mourning for the dead —
Henry Wadsworth Longfellow

Organic Inertia

Pinned against the ground's division
Of movement and stasis into a constant
Flux where one looks for signs of reason
In quivering green photosynthesis machines
Pumping waste at a gaseous expanse
Which coalesces as a cover
on the Earth an orphaned child,
The carbon hominids fret
At their diurnal need for urinals
Pair bonding and dead animals.
For death haunts every birth
And creation is destruction.

Aloft within the sky's dissection
Of void and alloyed cells' uncertain
Residence of terrains and oceans and all
Manner of interminglings between sustaining
The vacuum's voracious affirmation
That what lives it gives its tiny impetus,
Technohomosapiens flies
In triumph at Olympian heights
Blissfully dismissing the primal's time bomb tick.
For death haunts every birth
And creation is destruction.

Birthright

The rites of spring — our birthright of death in life
Greens the plains — drives the rains
Of hot wet death in life to lie
On mud suspended fields which yield
The green glow of open meadows
Life in death's shadow.

Manroot and Rosebud

I am the tree's veins plunging vainly
You are the ground's wet caked cracks.
I am the mountain's peak seeking heat
You are the clouds' supple molecules surrounding.
I am the geyser's joyous roaring bursts
You are the smiling sky opening wide.
I am the volcano pouring molten life force
You are the fields falling filled in its path.
I am the stem swaying in the wind's touch
You are the blossom in quivering bloom.
I am the ocean's all-enveloping calm
You are the oyster nestled contently on bottom.

Survival of the Litter Runt

To suck milk like a child
Hit the flat cracked ground
Teeter to your feet for a spot on teat
Battle blood sisters and brothers
To parasite off mother
In heat beating ceaselessly
On your back, your loin companions
Backs, Mother's back sagging
Under her burden, you're her burden, feel it
In paw swats on your sweating head
You slip from your spot on the teat
Emitting an animal wail from your vocal orifice
This is the moment of birth and death.

Severe Storm Warnings in Effect

creatures great
and small all
feel Earth's heat
and cold and waste
share the atmosphere
Adapt to persevere
the bitter weather
throws us all together

Natural Structure

Cave walls who soak hot Earth air
Pity us
Hard ground who cracks in dry caverns
Pity us
Gnarled trees who heave spastic epithets
Pity us
Raging rivers who handmaiden disease
Pity us

We created steel and concrete enclaves
To fight you
We molded wood and porcelain floors
To fight you
We painted pure and hybrid yields
To fight you
We boiled and sterilized threatening life
To fight you

Pity the stupidity of that creature, Man
Who can create a world beyond what Nature can

Life Expectancy

Homo Americanus emerges
In the sterile hospital
Then behind bars in a cradle.
Variable years in school
To labor in a cubicle
With the title of "Professional".
Then, content, full, and dull,
In pine or plastic, submerges

Corporate Park I

Princes, paupers
Bourgeois queens
The stench of wealth
Made by machines
And treating MAN
As mechanical, planned
Like some monkey
Hungry for money

As an empire
Of free men
We call sire
The scent of lucre
And treating MAN
Like he don't understand
We reap a yield
A plastic field

The Tenneco Tower Throws Cold Shadows

A face in the black-windowed wall
Wins a small victory
Hand-holding yuppie couples appalled
At their complicity
Ride the elevator
To the automatic teller.
Do Third World subsistence farmers
Harness electricity?

Crank Case

Here's a Hero's Welcome
To our Clone Culture
Hear the dynamo hum
Of a deity debacle
A dense fog of the random
Choking bourgeois men.
Call this autumnal chill
The Conformist's Hour of Lead
Transforming raw materials
Into empty hominid hungers.

American Trends: The End?

The industrialized world
Serves a platter of matter
To its origin: the depressed mass.
They feast on the abundance
Curse but accept the waste
Then let the unnatural swirl
Flush their minds —
They don't want to be left behind.

A Hungry Anger

My anger is a hard thing.
Touch it. Watch it stiffen
Then expand as a battering ram
Or power drill probing a hole
The kill, electric shrill
The metal. your flesh's rended tendons
Shards and sparks, your ego
Fragmented in the hollow
Left-over hole where
My anger's crammed, slammed
Repeat-
edly
Rhythm-
ically
Who you say
You are and who I am
All a jumble
Like an edible product's
Ingredient list.
Eat my anger and briefly deify
A sliver of my energy.
Feel it. It is a hard thing
And means to beat you till it wins.

The Science of Silence

Rancor and stupor share space
In a battle for balance
Heavy-lidded, pacified, I lie
On stone — ground and reformed
To yield clean ground.
I locomote bipedally across
This landscape haphazardly tossed
Down by Man with no grand plan
Other than use and waste —
Nothing I say will change this.

Knowledgeable Idiots

The pedagogue pores over ancient texts
Preserved detritus to dissect
The hand-scratched echoes of vocalizations
Become visual representations
Molded through repetition
Into utilitarian constellations
Of descriptions and abstractions.
So these little letters,
Bloated with Significance
Become his obsession
To the point of proudly yielding relevance
To only his inspection.
The expert reveling in
The greatest thrill — to possess
Flouting erudition
He forgot to process.

Encyclopedia Humanum is Missing Many Volumes

What's hard to understand
Is how fear robs us blind.

Feels Almost Human

This plastic is my constant friend
I seem to live to hold its hand
In it lies every fluid I use
In it lies every product I choose
Before this thing you call comfort
Each everything extracted hurt
Now demand commands the process
Of use excess waste and use.

Nothing Human Is Foreign to Me

There a man's hand
Worn by weary years
A thousand autos
And hominid automatons —
Confusion of creator and created.
I will buy a box of chocolates
And tampons and toilet paper perhaps.
I will read a good book
Then bleed dreaming of breeding.
You will hear me in a million motors' death chatter
And in the quiet of a clean commode.
There a woman's hand
White and smooth as tile will linger
Under hunger, under freed needs.

Hydrocarbon Blues

Plastic sacks, cuffs
And collar supports
Hangars, tapes
And microwave plates

Microorganisms
All around
No sight, schism
or sound

Behind the Register at a Convenience Store

Machines wrenched this ground
To mold a product mound
Swept clean, kept neat
So Homo Americanus greets
A tidy habitat
For his Maalox, Ex-Lax, and the like.
Behind the counter, lined in strict order
With a hominid's fastidious rigor
A cornucopia of Man-crated curatives —
What's in these plastics help him live.

Planned Obsolescence

Where fear and Nature
Are an attractive pair
Breathe air.
Where senses' essences
Are perpetually spent
Exhale there.
Peacefully believe in abstract Care.
Here is not where
The machine engine of human anatomy
Breaks.

Wooden Man

Wood adrift
Floats purposeless.
The Hows of Formation
The Whys of destination
Not ingrained.
Battered and beaten
It threatens to splinter
In the rising tide's
Mindless surge.
Helplessly bobbing'
In hopeless ignorance
Awaiting decay

Infinite Sameness

Bored carnivores
Lounge on a plain.
They shat and ate
Then humped their mate.
In a reflex yawn
They gather extra oxygen
And wait until their satiation
Dissipates.

Then boredom returns.

Desperate Stairs

In every brick cave
A heart beats safe
Hear their breath fill the air.
By every soft bedside
An animal hides
See their fear thrill and dare.
To lie still beside you
With the world out of view
Feel desperate in its stare.

Innocent Piss

Failure to crawl
For the small child
Signifies all.
Lack of locomotion
Breed bad emotion
He grimaces at the waste.

Hear him scream.
He knows only his needs.
Nutrients for his nuclei
Random visual stimuli
Pacifies.

Fear to die, fear to die.

A Unique Vision?

Oblique, the obliging freak,
Squints as the glint
From his visions rosy tint
Hints at stints of mind manipulation,
Winks as he thinks his investigations
Will find his mind leaving behind deprivation.
For he leaks weak fragments when he speaks
And, believe, he is not so unique.

Speechless Statis Slept Here

So I sit here, watching Western ways decay
Time's always certain uncertainty
Displacing this place, conditioned, partitioned,
In the catharsis of stasis
What is is, stagnant incarnate
A billion limbs, slim and limber
Fat and taut as timber
Both locomote and deteriorate
Inarticulate.

Crummy Rummage

Voices honeycomb
Choices for the numb
Strangers' anger bleeds
On clean plates where I feed.
The dissected succumb
To my organic needs
The crumbs, the grubby crumbs
A rummage sale of seed

We Walk the Line

One moment everything is nothing
The next, it is all
Primates live in a linear reality
Not some misapplied Einsteinian
Time flux — yeah, it sucks
But consumptive intervals
Are simple and natural
Accept that it is
Then reject this —
You've still earned a formal burial

Fear Reified

She held an emptiness
Food could never fill
A desperation friction only intensified
A bond with a void she deified
Her organic wick sizzled with sickness
Its charred horror held that emptiness
At last in warm caress
Her life snuffed
Like mangled candles

Microorganisms

In the open spaces, space opens
To encompass the pompous and base
A canvas beyond mortal Ken
does exist, though it wears a false face.
A sick mystic statistic
In the ledger of Man's adaptations.

Still they use a urinal
And swill thee chemical, alcohol
Worship the artificial
Over the rougher Natural
Its violence makes them seem ill
But all creatures in Nature
From parasites to hominidae's haughty heights
Kill, they kill, all animals kill
All animals kill.

Psychomachea

(for Wendy Greiner)

Gold chains and blond strands descend
Gracefully to the nape of her neck
But fungal growths and ruptured veins
Map reality more mimetically.
Her scars are Desire's angels
I live for a shot of her snot
To playfully fluff her dandruff
Then watch her squat
Her urine sweet syrup to me —
I accept the waste of her body
As sacrament and liturgy.

What the Bible Contains

It fills the memory
With a paradise of glory
Its precepts bind
Our good — the design
The soldier's sword —
Here paradise is restored

White Witch Hollow

Yes, Yes, your eyes lie:
The sparkle of a dark witch
Your eyes lie
In volumes that fill rooms
Your eyes lie
Like spit and shit between the temples
Your eyes lie
The vicious disease of stupidity
Your eyes lie
Mine shafted — hollow bottomed
Your eyes lie
Forge steel cleats of deceit
Your eyes lie
But they sleep soundly
For they're empty, empty, empty
Like their loving owner
Who deserves to die
Yes, Yes, your eyes lie
Beside you now
White witch hollow

Manufactured Disaster

At Hunter's Chase Road and Technology Boulevard
The hills are high as Man's will
His products strewn in shards
Where the intersection meets to tame
Our interaction
The prescription for disaster
Glows on these bits of plaster
Find a product to market
Then jump in the jungle
The tangle of angles
Still revolves around the selfish
Intersections tame our interactions
The prescription for disaster
Glows on these bits of plaster
We want to own our own home
So no one knows our habits
Except our possessed mates
Who reel in shared wealth
In this artificial habitat
Electricity mastered at your fingertips
And food a frozen closet away
The walls — tastefully decorated
Don't forget to hate
The prescription for disaster
Glows on these bits of plaster

The Established Couple

As solitary as a nun's DNA,
We kneel in these putrid pews
Out of habit — nude
As two tropical castaways
Bored with each other's company.
We know all we need to know
And so we act blank
Uncomfortably stuck in love's elevator —
A long drop from the top
Or any heavenly reach — your hand's touch
Makes my flesh retch and twitch
In undulating repulsion.
You are sick of it, you say.
So you too piss in the pew
And stain the hymnal with frustration.

Emergence as Raw Experience

We learn to care.
Taught by distraught
Mothers smothering
Our forms in warm
Embraces. Our faces
Are genetically set
In simian similarity. And yet
We each can reach
Toward another for comfort
Without things
Inhibiting our habitation
Of peaceful satiation.
But sometimes without
Rhyme
We forget and hate.

What Means Much

She held him in a limbo
Arms all akimbo
The false mutterings of dunces
Who only loved her parts
Had no inkling her heart
Was silken fabric waiting for a soft touch
Of utopian cloaking
From the world of male gang violence
And fights to the death for dominance.

She prefers security
A loving hug that tugs her toward
Words of absurd faith
In simple animal clutches
Which mean so much, so much.

On the Creation of Artificial Environments

Hominids hid from the land —
A random hand
Of harsh forces torching
Their brief wick of organic
Sustenance sustained by waste.
One taste of safety
And Man began to plan
His habitats — [not happenstance adaptations
To wild environmental
Conditions but creation]?
Of spacious niches
He could control.
Their proliferation — Man's prime manipulation
Witness Homo Americanus
His air — temperately conditioned
Dead food in an Arctic approximation
Endless stimulus and inter-tribal communication
Through an electromagnetic presentation
Hominidae achieves satiation.

The Conversion of Wallace Stevens

On your deathbed, you lied
The facts you knew
You tried to hide
Your idea of order
Died — it died and try
As you might your wish
Was your life, denied.
Ramon Fernandez, tell me why
Idols and icons and dreams
Can guarantee eternity
When you must see that be
Be finale of seem and be.
To be is all all is.
I know you knew but you
Were you — I am me and
It will never be said.
That on my deathbed, I lied.

The Consent of the Governed

The soaringly surreal scarlet bogies
Down my rear windshield they gleefully bear
Like a hellhound suspended in mid-air
Violating Newtonian theory
Laws they embody; for truth they don't care
With my civil disobedient dare
I challenge their rightful authority
Unknown force like lead on my driving foot
Onward I ride striking blows for freedom
Bullets sing by like tearing eagle claws
Our seed, wealth, robes, and arms used to put
Marchers, tax dodgers rotting in prison
My duty's to disobey unjust laws.

The American Way!

Down in the street at four in the morning
Darkness escapes — the day is a-borning!
Errol Flynn's down there, looking for a Jap spy,
Close the blinds, dear, you're making me cry.
Here in Hawaii it's the witching hour,
And Errol's off in the bushes with Tyrone Power.
Errol moved the movie here so he could take pictures
Of gun emplacements and aircraft fixtures.
Sure, he took drugs,
You worthlessly poor, glamour-struck slugs.
But that's okay
It's only the American Way!
Can I stand to see my heroes so stripped?
Somehow it screws up my idol worship.
Errol Flynn a Nazi — lover of kamikases?
Next you'll tell me John Wayne was a Commie.
But it takes True Grit to battle cancer and die
So he'll always be somewhat special in my eyes.
Still, I watch his movies like a firefly eats her mate,
When I see him zap Japs, my heart feels great,
My mind wells with prefabricated hate.
An American hero for my American tastes.

Sister Cindy

Sister Cindy, with your tattered flasher coat,
Scraggly hair like the bard of a billy goat,
Ski slope nose under ice blue eyes,
Preaching screeching diatribes under darkening skies.
The sinners stroll by, some stop to listen,
As you try to save them from the sin of fornication.
Women are sluts, men are operators,
What makes you so despise fornicators?
Did your Daddy once knock on your pink bedroom door,
And crawl across the Snow White throw rug on the floor
To plow into you to deflower your box,
As the hour struck midnight from the church's chiming clock?
Now no one wants to give you the rod,
So every evening you're rammed by God.
You clutch your hat, legs straight in the air,
The two of you make an attractive pair.
Your jagged mouth screaming bitter words of hate,
Making everyone realize how God's love is great.

The Status Quo is my Hero

I just love the way of the world
The way of all flesh, the way it is.
Encephalitic brains, political campaigns
Sparkling champagne without the fizz.
Whiteheads, blackheads, warheads, lead
Lethal injections, viral infections
Romantic rejections, Immaculate Conception
The Cult of the Virgin, tonic and gin
Rambunctious Reverends, original sin
Drunk drivers, dental pliers
Treadless tires, castrati choirs
Wishbones, the "unknown"
Breath mints, lighter flints
Skin cancer, topless dancers
Lent, lint, nuclear winter
Indian Summer, Niagara Falls
The inner planets, the outer giants
W and Y particles, neutrinos and quarks
The elements, public works
The Universe, the Curse
Bleeding, breeding, feeding
Civil strife, the Gift of Life
Yes, I want a hero — not an uncommon
want — an unrealistic one.
Better to be a hero
Revel in your ego
Adore the status quo
This is the way the world is
A Big Bang and a shrimp whimper
Sharing the same space

The Order of Things

Perfection is momentary pleasure.
Pleasure is momentary perfection.
Pinpoint for a moment
Your loquacious displacement.
Why you still scrawl on parchment
For the sake of chaff salvation,
When order constructs itself
From a pile of dry ideals.

The Condemned Complex

This building, my hands
Aimed to etch, came to watch
My sensations dissipate,
My will to feel stolen.
These walls were my canvas.
The lumps and air bubbles — my refracted reflection.
The distraction of asphyxiation
Never bothered me. I breathed
A rarefied air of inability anyway.
I overheard the jostling molecules
Mocking Michelangelo, talking of me
Screaming in silent synesthesia
My apologia for existing.
While the skeletal easel melted
Into this witches brew
Of feelings I vomit
And in gagging on, renew.

The Wave

(for Jackie Painter)

The empty aching image
Of your slowly breaking smile
Explodes over my mind,
A wave of saving knowledge
Still haunted by the miles
That tally every gesture
Color every idle thought,
The water flows through,
Thrills my gills,
The throat of heart caught
By the choking air I must caress
My arms stroking the emptiness.

The Hairy Ape

(for Nelson Barquet RIP)

"Tinkin', Tinkin'" he says with a swagger
The tinkling clink of swizzle sticks and glass
Accompanying in 4/4 time — all time —
His musings on the sixth or seventh swallowed jigger.
Molasses streams of people pass
Cackling, mocking the insights of rhyme.
Yet he, now on eight, stares down at his leg,
Notices fur, then wiggles his toes
Which resemble a prehensile tail.
And his arm, a brutish construction,
Not a poetic rhyme scheme, deliberate,
But developmental. It allows lofty thought
Beyond the squirrel sucking sustenance from a nut,
But no explanation for this obvious
creation — the greatest deception.

The Reigning Monarch

Let the soft drops sprinkle tingling touches
On the random exposed appendages of my body.
Let the ants scurry on cement and concrete
Eager to escape the growing liquid tapestry.
Let the twisted tree reach dystrophic limbs
Toward a sky providing life and the only mystery.
Let the water not stop falling, for I refuse
To rise and fall. The breath of my chest may heave
A convulsive accordion accompanying these thoughts.
But breath and thought do not make me believe
What I know has never been, and is not.

Another Cold Soldier

Darkness still covered like
the covers we wore
that stripped the human
Negatives we share
Shored against a storm
That ticked precariously
Against the porous screen
We allowed between us
Another cold soldier
Awaiting a sign or order
That he march forward
He remembers letters
Redolent of roses
Home in some houses
She slips off her hose
He buried his nose
Now blown
A sudden searing silo
Into the rank trench
His groaning soars
A gaping open mouth
Raining in iridescent splendor
Into the night sky

Black Beauty

Into the field I turned left
Spotting the mottled horse hopping
Down the dirt path. He kept
One delicate hoof crinkled like
A fountain statue or a bike's
Broken spoke. I watched him laughing
"That will be good leg for chopping."

I stick his hind leg down into
The pick-up truck. It starts without
Fail. The hand painted lettering "Glue"
Blends warmly with the aqua-marine-baby
Blue background. Maybe,
I tell myself, the horse didn't shout
And I've never seen birds fly south.

Teasing

Limb from limb: he screamed
Indistinguishable
Swirling ceiling windmills
Cartwheel and reassemble
Into supple plump pillows
With pert buttons
She stands before the bathroom mirror
Stroking the subtly wrinkled areola
Dreaming of a human touch
Or humane treatment

Disneyland of Death

Two minutes amid
The weeping, wailing
And gnashing of teeth
Will silence your lying cry
Forever.
The perfume of putrid epidermis
Singes your nostril hairs.
Drink the wine of God's wrath
Inebriate of Air:
It's a Disneyland of Death
Where the fireworks never end
But explode in your hand
At three, six, and ten.
But at eleven
Behind Seven-Eleven
You slam the last six-pack
And watch the bobbing goddess
Gag and gurgle on your bottle
Then stop abruptly.
You cry aloud in agony,
"Too late, too late."

In the American Train

(dedicated to William Carlos Williams)

America
is trains.
Train:
Pulling Pullman sleepers
Bound for vaudeville towns
Stars yet undiscovered
Singing in the aisle
While
Their father contracts small-pox.

Baby dripping shit
Onto a plastic potty
Ronald McDonald's hat.

A line of
Large black acrobats
Repeatedly raping
A lily-white liberty belle
Sticking snowflake earrings sideways
Up her crack.

A Little Like Hilarity Hall

Laugh: Let it out!
Chuckle, cackle
Giggle, guffaw!
Alleviate anxiety!
Drain depression!
Emotional expression
Never hurt anyone!
Carry a smile and
The smile carries you!
Biofeedback works!
Sense pleasures are
A fingertip away!
Don't allow your heartfelt touch
to decay.
You are happy.
You are good.
Your life has meaning and order.

Nutty

In cold I shiver
In heat I quiver
To horizon's elemental poison.
The physics of a lever
To pry my psychic fever
Illuminates my disturbed effluvium.
Theatric vocablic mask
Behind waxes ashen
My mind melted putty.
Mommy, come here hold me
I know only what you called me
Nutty — Nutty silly putty
But bloody, mama bloody brain
Breathing earthly energy.

The "Great Apes" of History

All primates make political alliances.
It's true. If you
Don't believe me,
Read the histories.
The "Great Apes" especially shine.
Their lives, their loves, their
Visions beyond pro-simian kind
Kind of make up the story.
If they possess
Political finesse
They rise to the top of the tree
Effortlessly.
Unless, of course, they're terrestrial
As all primates are
Eventually.

Economic Reality

NBC-TV treats
Texas cattlebuyers
As obscene freaks,
Carnival sideshows
Of the gaudy gross.
The beer-bellied steelworker
Bloated over his belt
Laughs aloud
For the first time
Since he lost his wife.

On Killing Living Things

How morality entered the picture
I'll never understand. It split the screen
Between the higher order of mammal
Utilizing cognitive compassion
And the short nasty brute no better than
The animal he callously kills. Well,
I sit here with a beer watching T.V.
And the scene I'm seeing does appall me.
Monkeys wiggle on unsterile tables
As hammers crush their fragile eggshell skulls.
But bring this act into clearer focus.
All natural law is artificial.
Survival governs every living thing.
As the swordfish swallows minnows so that
The species prospers, so right and wrong are
Mental constructs with no relation to
Man-kind manhandling subordinate
Animals. Supposedly morality
Stops our intra-species self-destruction,
But the next story I see tells me
That animal rights activists killed three
People by blowing up a lab they said
Engaged in unbelievable cruelty,
And they were outraged.

Rack 'Em Up

Let me buy you another drink, Dick
No need now to stop
Look at that hot, big-titted chick
With the lacy, see through top
Look at her buy those phallic cigarettes
I know what they're for
She sure deserves whatever she gets
She's just a sleazy whore
Ha! Harry's stopping her at the bar
What's he gonna do?
Don't let the bitch get back to her car!
We're all right behind you
Throw her on the center pool table
Spread her legs outwide
The cunt just called us lowlife rabble
We'll give her a free ride
Drop her pants down to her knees
Tie her with her belt
Pound the pud in her dry crease
But don't mess up the table's felt
Grab your beers and get in line
To pop your plug in the socket
I'm sure she likes it just fine
8-ball in the corner pocket
When you're through — just let her go
Let her try and hide
Her deepest secret, we all know
She's glad we came inside

Sermons on the Random

Sixty-six mules try mind manipulation.

A melodic fragment
From a hard-cover, educationally-approved
Sixth-grade text — red, white, and blue
All over — not a newspaper
A lie is a lie is a lie.
Only churches have children's choirs
The school singers sing in rounds
"America, the Beautiful," "Row, Row Your Boat"
What about the Erie Canal?

It's like they said when we were kids.

Her daughter flaunts her bedbug bites
Ruby birthstones
She groans alone tonight at home.
Her mother checks coats at the club
During a debutante dance.
She
Jumps the bridge
Water jumps to meet her
A sliding glass door
Straight to inferno
She brakes.

I turn back to face me but I'm already there.

A melancholy, brooding, (pompous), lad
Often calmed by evening half-drunken blind
With rage; who, in his own opinion, had
Fried his mind when the light of knowledge shined
Off the pavement, through the glass, magnified
A thousand times; he can never return
To the flat earth he left so far behind
When first wit's sun slowly started burning
What else can he learn?

It's like they said when we were kids.

The bar back rack holds cold brew
And I hold you
A voice speaks of no choice, no view,
As I told you
The walls dissolve in unmarked graves
The tile floor rips
I hold a broken bottle inches above
Your exposed ribs

I turn back to face me but I'm already there.

I believe you
Because the other kids
Can never know how
I hide at night
The family fights
I quietly listen
The screams sweep upstairs
To clean my ears
My brother beats my mother
In the face with a frying pan
I can't cry, can't face
The bitter cacophony
My home a hall of ignominy
My room a gallery of impotency
I paint pained portraits
That eye my futile worry
I hear the car
Hurry out the driveway
I flake back the blind
In time to see my Father
Pulling away
I wish I was.

Let's forget about ourselves and magnify the Lord and worship him! As a faith partner you too can share with my Father and I when I deliver us from my daily sermon right here on your Christian network and if you act now I will send you one of my Jesus First Lapel Pins which you can proudly wear like stigmata — A red badge of courage. We'll pay for the call.

It's like they said when we were kids.

The Literature of Exhaustion

The air was cold.
Steak chunks splatter rented furniture
I like a look of Agony

Why am I writing? I've nothing to say.

Cold was the air.
The wood is stained with blow
Two roads diverged in a yellow wood

Was the air cold?
A cornucopia of colors crowns the cushions
Mighty Casey has struck out.

I'm exhausted with literature — this is ridiculous

It means something to me

The cold air was — that's all that matters.

Author's Biography:

PoetKen Jones was born a cis-normative upper middle class white male who now self-identifies as an intersectional cross-species activist after successful oral and physical discourse with multiple pussy ... cats.

Photo by MLH

For more information:
www.poetken.com
or poetken@yahoo.com